SE 1 9

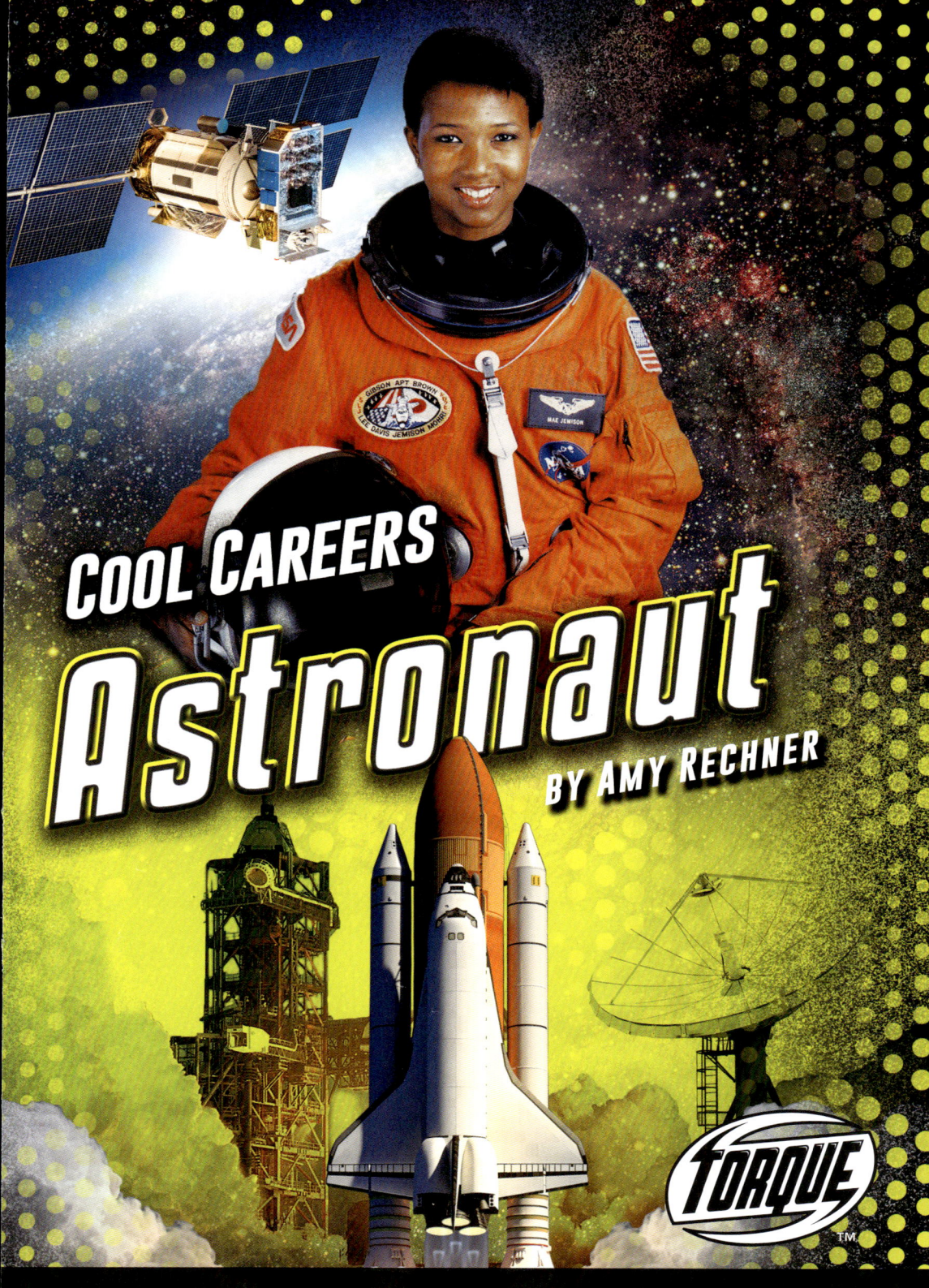

Are you ready to take it to the extreme? Torque books thrust you into the action-packed world of sports, vehicles, mystery, and adventure. These books may include dirt, smoke, fire, and dangerous stunts.

WARNING: read at your own risk.

This edition first published in 2020 by Bellwether Media, Inc.

No part of this publication may be reproduced in whole or in part without written permission of the publisher. For information regarding permission, write to Bellwether Media, Inc., Attention: Permissions Department, 6012 Blue Circle Drive, Minnetonka, MN 55343.

Library of Congress Cataloging-in-Publication Data

Names: Rechner, Amy, author.
Title: Astronaut / by Amy Rechner.
Description: Minneapolis, MN : Bellwether Media, Inc., [2020] | Series: Torque. Cool Careers | Audience: Ages 7-12. | Includes bibliographical references and index.
Identifiers: LCCN 2018061281 (print) | LCCN 2019000716 (ebook) | ISBN 9781618916273 (ebook) | ISBN 9781644870600 (hardcover : alk. paper)
Subjects: LCSH: Astronautics–Vocational guidance–Juvenile literature. | Astronauts–Juvenile literature.
Classification: LCC TL793 (ebook) | LCC TL793 .R43 2020 (print) | DDC 629.450023–dc23
LC record available at https://lccn.loc.gov/2018061281

Text copyright © 2020 by Bellwether Media, Inc. TORQUE and associated logos are trademarks and/or registered trademarks of Bellwether Media, Inc. SCHOLASTIC, CHILDREN'S PRESS, and associated logos are trademarks and/or registered trademarks of Scholastic Inc., 557 Broadway, New York, NY 10012.

Editor: Kate Moening   Designer: Josh Brink

TABLE OF CONTENTS

Out of This World 4

Scientists of the Stars 6

Astronauts in Training 12

Future Astronauts Wanted! 18

Glossary 22

To Learn More 23

Index 24

Out of This World

Buzz! An alarm wakes the astronaut. She has been asleep standing up, held up by her sleeping bag. There is very little **gravity**. She floats out of the bag and pushes off the walls with her feet.

The astronaut is conducting science experiments today! She is studying how space changes the human senses. She also helps keep the **International Space Station** (ISS) working properly.

SUNRISE, SUNSET

The ISS flies past 16 sunrises and 16 sunsets as it zooms around Earth!

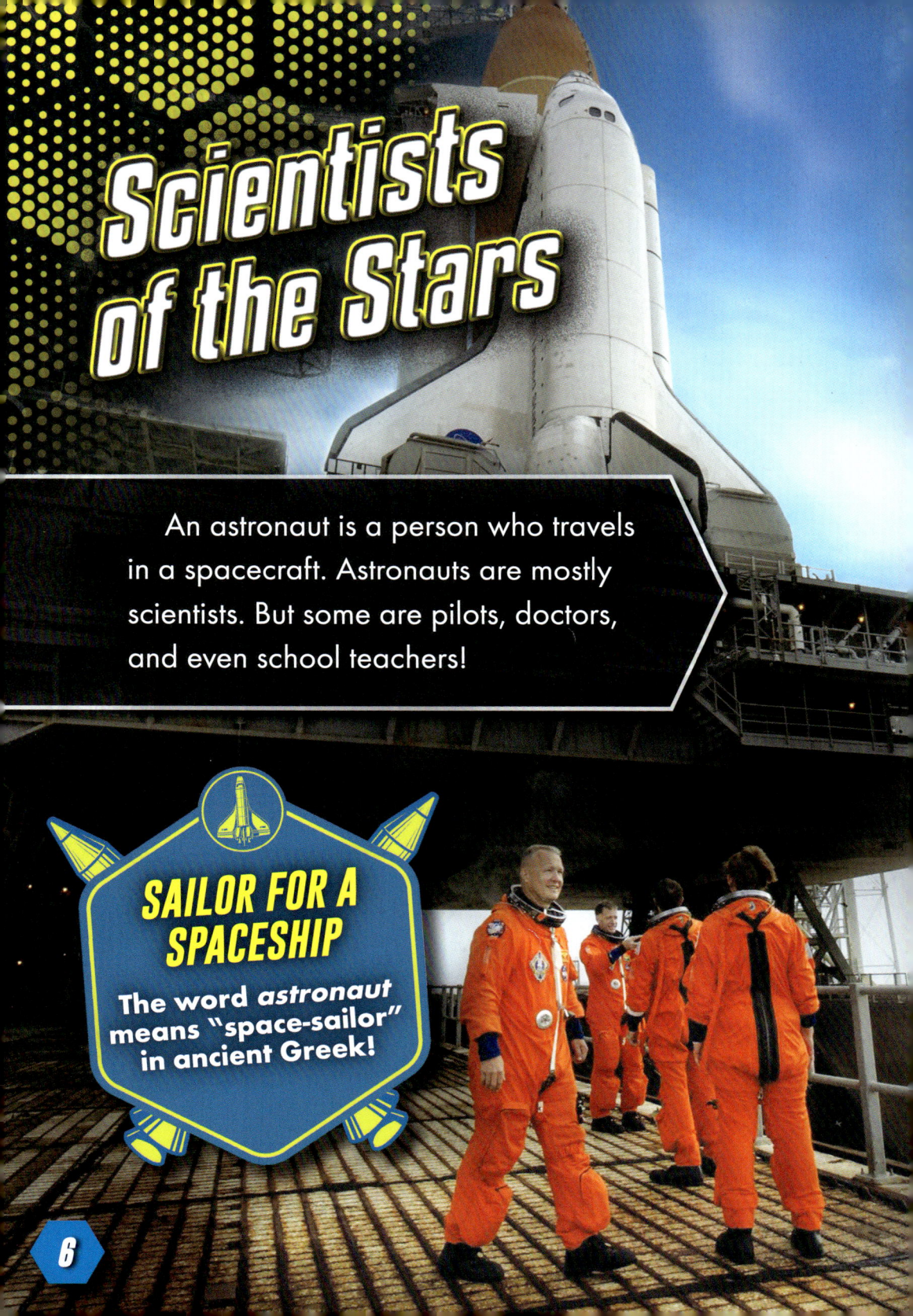

Scientists of the Stars

An astronaut is a person who travels in a spacecraft. Astronauts are mostly scientists. But some are pilots, doctors, and even school teachers!

SAILOR FOR A SPACESHIP

The word *astronaut* means "space-sailor" in ancient Greek!

The United States government established **NASA** in 1958. The job of astronaut was created a year later. The first astronauts were pilots and **engineers**. Some worked with NASA's scientists to build spacecraft.

Most astronaut crews fly **missions** to the ISS. Their missions last about six months. Russian **cosmonauts** and astronauts from other countries are also on the crews.

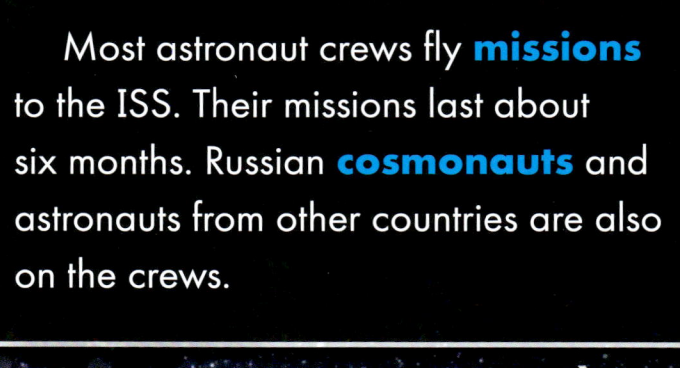

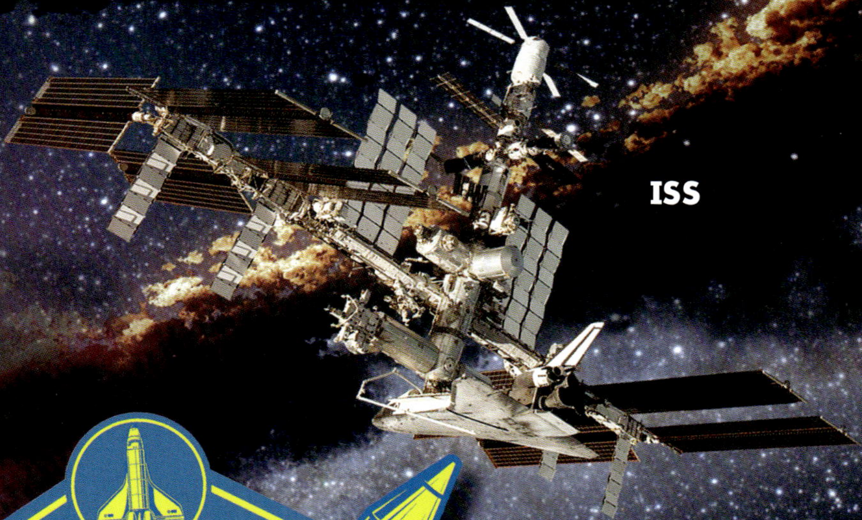

ISS

SPEEDING THROUGH SPACE

Soyuz spacecraft reach outer space in minutes. But they take several days to catch the ISS. The ISS flies 17,000 miles (27,359 kilometers) per hour!

Soyuz

The ISS **orbits** Earth from about 240 miles (386 kilometers) away. It gives astronauts a safe place to live and work. Astronauts get to the ISS on Russian spacecraft called Soyuz. The Soyuz also carry supplies like food and medicine.

The ISS is a giant science lab. It is about the size of a football field!

Many science experiments happen on the ISS. Astronauts observe changes to Earth's **climate**. They study the effects of zero gravity on the human body and plant life.

experiment on ISS

Famous Face
Sunita (Suni) Williams

BORN: SEPTEMBER 19, 1965

HOMETOWN: NEEDHAM, MASSACHUSETTS

EDUCATION:
- PHYSICAL SCIENCE DEGREE (U.S. NAVAL ACADEMY)
- ENGINEERING MANAGEMENT DEGREE (FLORIDA INSTITUTE OF TECHNOLOGY)

PREVIOUS EXPERIENCE: U.S. NAVY TEST PILOT

ACHIEVEMENTS:
- 322 DAYS IN SPACE ON TWO MISSIONS
- 4 SPACEWALKS OUTSIDE THE ISS
- CHOSEN FOR THE CREW OF A SPACECRAFT BUILT BY THE BOEING COMPANY, AN IMPORTANT EXPERIMENT FOR FUTURE SPACE TRAVEL

Sunita Williams

Astronauts in Training

Most of an astronaut's time is spent on Earth. Training for space travel takes a long time. Astronauts study space station systems, robotic operations, and the Russian language.

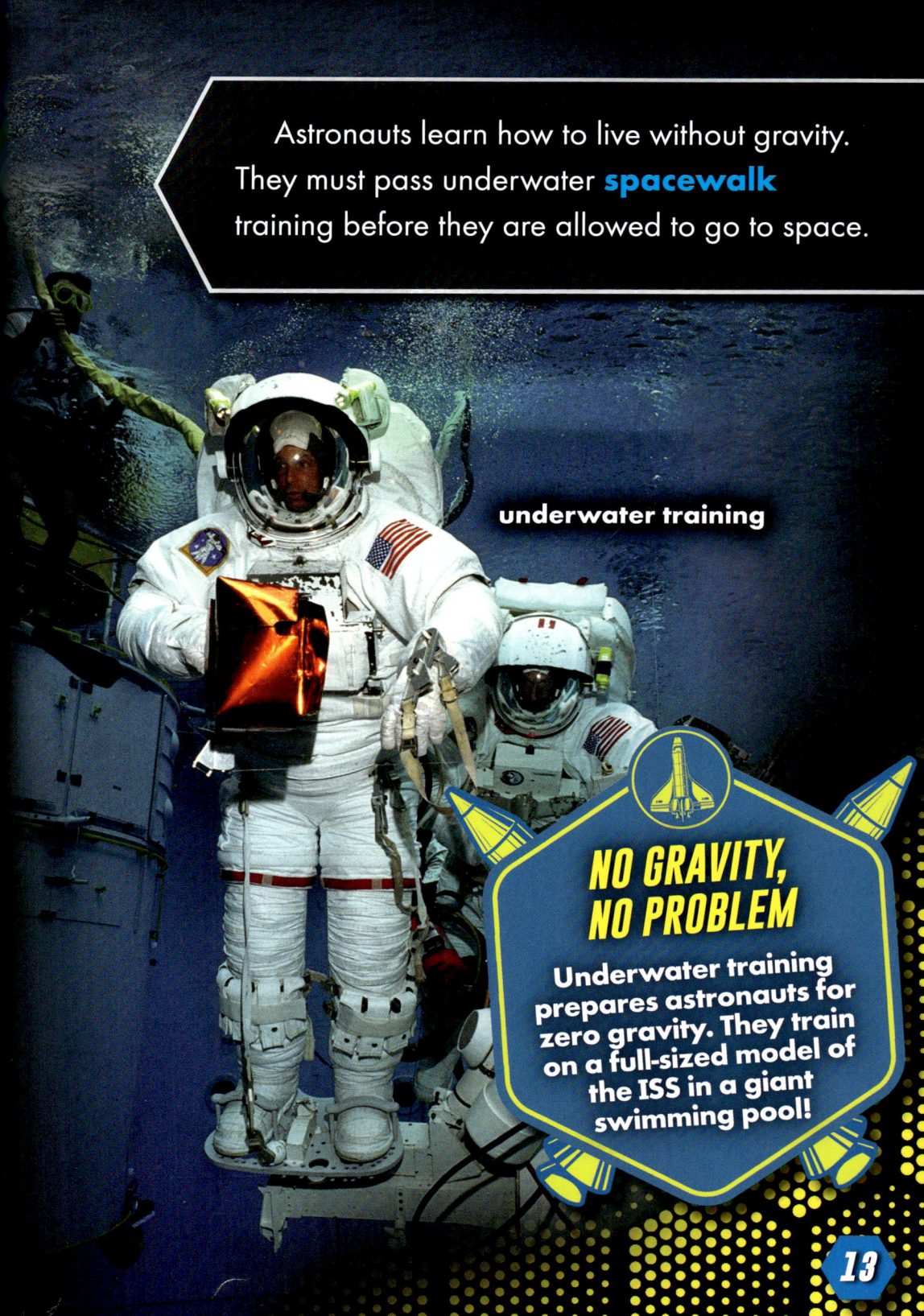

Astronauts learn how to live without gravity. They must pass underwater **spacewalk** training before they are allowed to go to space.

underwater training

NO GRAVITY, NO PROBLEM

Underwater training prepares astronauts for zero gravity. They train on a full-sized model of the ISS in a giant swimming pool!

NASA has many jobs for astronauts. Some work on Earth in **mission control**. They talk to crews in orbit. Engineers create systems to make space travel easier. Astronauts on active duty continue training. Astronauts in space conduct many experiments!

Many people help plan future missions. Astronauts want to visit other planets and build new space stations.

Vomit Comet training plane

VOMIT COMET

Astronauts train in a special plane that swoops quickly. It lets them feel zero gravity! It often makes trainees throw up, so they call it the Vomit Comet.

ISS Workday Checklist

- ☑ **6:00 AM:** WAKE UP! USE A SOAPY CLOTH TO BATHE

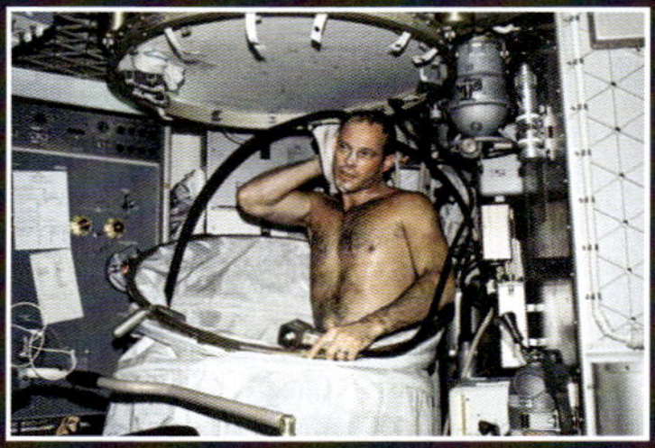

- ☑ **8:00 AM:** VIDEO CHECK-IN WITH MISSION CONTROL

- ☑ **8:15 AM:** WORK ON EXPERIMENTS AND MAINTENANCE

- ☑ **11:45 AM:** EXERCISE

- ☑ **2:00 PM:** MORE WORK TIME

- ☑ **5:30 PM:** MORE EXERCISE

- ☑ **7:00 PM:** FREE TIME!

- ☑ **9:30 PM:** BEDTIME

15

WHAT A WORKOUT!

Space travel is hard on the human body! Astronauts must exercise for about two hours each day to stay strong.

Astronaut safety is a huge task. Engineers and astronauts work together to update spacesuits. Spacesuits must keep astronauts safe from **extreme** temperatures, space dust, and other dangers.

In space, a team works on the robotic arm outside the ISS to keep it working safely. Astronauts operate the arm to grab spacecraft and connect the spacecraft to the station. Sometimes they do spacewalks to fix the arm.

spacewalk

Future Astronauts Wanted!

Tomorrow's astronauts will discover new worlds. Getting there will take a lot of work! Astronauts must have a good education. They must be strong leaders who stay calm under pressure.

Astronauts share a tiny space for many months. They have to be team players. They must be able work out their problems fairly.

Astronaut Wanted!

SOMEONE WHO WILL REACH FOR THE STARS!

EDUCATION: COLLEGE DEGREE IN SCIENCE, MATH, OR COMPUTERS

EXPERIENCE: SEVERAL YEARS IN SCIENCE-RELATED FIELD OR MILITARY FLYING EXPERIENCE

QUALITIES:
- GREAT TEAM PLAYERS
- STRONG LEADERS
- GOOD COMMUNICATORS
- IN EXCELLENT SHAPE WITH PERFECT VISION: GLASSES OK

SALARIES FOR THIS POSITION CAN REACH $150,000!

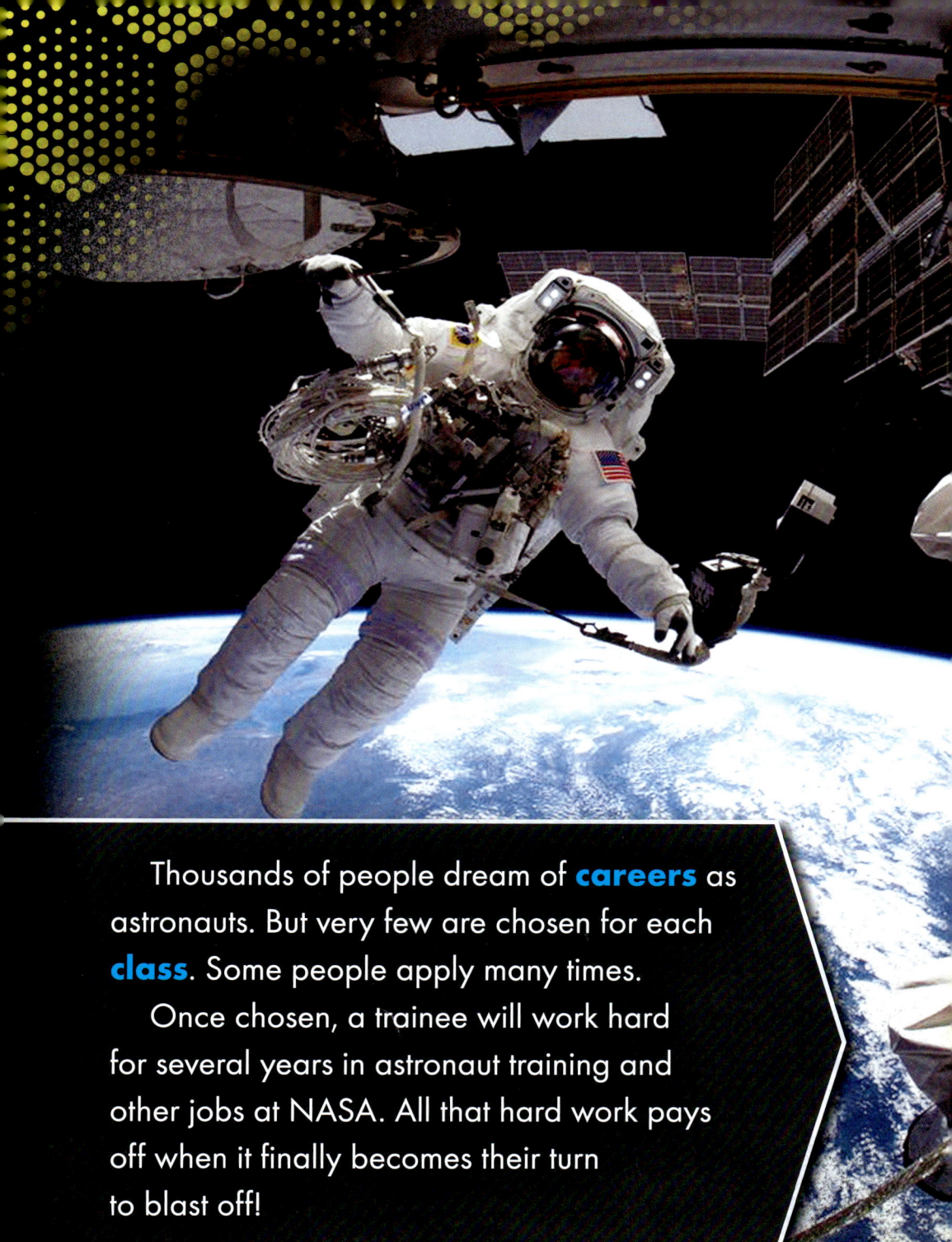

Thousands of people dream of **careers** as astronauts. But very few are chosen for each **class**. Some people apply many times.

Once chosen, a trainee will work hard for several years in astronaut training and other jobs at NASA. All that hard work pays off when it finally becomes their turn to blast off!

Career Path

COLLEGE 4-6 YEARS

IN A JOB 3+ YEARS, OR 1000 FLIGHT HOURS

TRAINING 2 YEARS; WAIT FOR MISSION

SELECTED FOR MISSION

TRAIN ABOUT 3 YEARS

BLAST OFF!

Glossary

careers—jobs people do for a long time

class—a group of astronauts chosen to train at the same time

climate—the long-term weather conditions in a certain area

cosmonauts—Russian astronauts

engineers—people who design and build spacecraft and other machines

extreme—the highest or lowest possible

gravity—the natural force that makes things fall toward Earth

International Space Station—a place for astronauts from all over the world to work in outer space

mission control—a center at NASA that manages space flights from launch to landing

missions—projects that are assigned to astronaut crews to complete in space

NASA—National Aeronautics and Space Administration; NASA is a U.S. government agency responsible for space travel and exploration.

orbits—moves in a circle around something

spacewalk—a movement outside a spacecraft by an astronaut

To Learn More

AT THE LIBRARY

Gitlin, Marty. *Careers in Personal Space Travel*. Ann Arbor, Mich.: Cherry Lake Publishing, 2019.

Morey, Allan. *The International Space Station*. Minneapolis, Minn.: Bellwether Media, 2018.

Williams, Dave, and Loredana Cunti. *Go for Liftoff: How to Train Like an Astronaut*. Toronto, Ont.: Annick Press, 2017.

ON THE WEB

FACTSURFER

Factsurfer.com gives you a safe, fun way to find more information.

1. Go to www.factsurfer.com.

2. Enter "astronaut" into the search box and click.

3. Select your book cover to see a list of related web sites.

Index

career path, 21
careers, 20
class, 20
climate, 10
cosmonauts, 8
Earth, 5, 9, 10, 12, 14
education, 18
engineers, 7, 14, 16
exercise, 16
experiments, 5, 10, 14
gravity, 4, 10, 13, 14
International Space Station, 5, 8, 9, 10, 13, 17
ISS workday checklist, 15
job posting, 19
mission control, 14
missions, 8, 14
NASA, 7, 14, 20
orbits, 9, 14
pilots, 6, 7
robotic arm, 17
safety, 16, 17
scientists, 6, 7
Soyuz, 8, 9
spacecraft, 6, 7, 8, 9, 17
spacesuits, 16
spacewalk, 13, 17
training, 12, 13, 14, 20
United States, 7
Vomit Comet, 14
Williams, Sunita, 11

The images in this book are reproduced through the courtesy of: NASA Gov, front cover (hero), pp. 10, 13, 14, 15, 16, 18, 19, 20, 21 (top right, middle left, middle right, bottom left, bottom right); 3DSculptor, front cover (shuttle launch); NASA Johnson/ NASA Flickr, pp. 4, 5; NASA HQ/ NASA Flickr, pp. 6, 7, 9, 17, 18; NikoNomad, p. 8; Bricktop/ Wiki Commons, p. 11; Kurun/ Wiki Commons, p. 12; g-stockstudio, p. 21 (top left).